JUNIOR BIOS

T0019954

Zoë Kravitz

BY NORA GARDINER

Enslow
PUBLISHING

Please visit our website, www.enslow.com. For a free color catalog of all our high-quality books, call toll free 1-800-398-2504 or fax 1-877-980-4454.

Library of Congress Cataloging-in-Publication Data

Names: Gardiner, Nora, author.
Title: Zoë Kravitz / Nora Gardiner.
Description: New York : Enslow Publishing, 2022. | Series: Junior bios | Includes bibliographical references, webliography, index.
Identifiers: LCCN 2020033820 | ISBN 9781978522602 (library binding) | ISBN 9781978522589 (paperback) | ISBN 9781978522596 (6 pack) | ISBN 9781978522619 (ebook)
Subjects: LCSH: Kravitz, Zoë, 1988—Juvenile literature. | Actors—United States—Biography. | Singers—United States—Biography—Juvenile literature.
Classification: LCC PN2287.K73 G37 2022 | DDC 791.4302/8092 [B]—dc23
LC record available at https://lccn.loc.gov/2020033820

First Edition

Published in 2022 by
Enslow Publishing
29 E. 21st Street
New York, NY 10010

Designer: Deanna Paternostro
Editor: Kate Mikoley

Photo credits: Cover, p. 1 (Zoë Kravitz) Amy Sussman/Staff/Getty Images Entertainment/Getty Images; cover, p. 1 (photo frame) Aleksandr Andrushkiv/Shutterstock.com; marble texture used throughout HardtIllustrations/Shutterstock.com; lined paper texture used throughout Mtsaride/Shutterstock.com; watercolor texture used throughout solarbird/Shutterstock.com; p. 5 Axelle/Bauer-Griffin/Contributor/FilmMagic/Getty Images; p. 7 Kevork Djansezian/Stringer/Getty Images Entertainment/Getty Images; p. 9 Murray Close/Contributor/Moviepix/Getty Images; p. 11 Steve Granitz/Contributor/WireImage/Getty Images; p. 13 Jeff Kravitz/Contributor/FilmMagic, Inc./Getty Images; p. 15 Jason Merritt/TERM/Staff/Getty Images Entertainment/Getty Images; p. 16 Steven Ferdman/Stringer/Getty Images Entertainment/Getty Images; p. 17 John Phillips/Stringer/Getty Images Entertainment/Getty Images; p. 19 Mike Marsland/Contributor/WireImage/Getty Images.

Printed in the United States of America

CPSIA compliance information: Batch #CSENS22: For further information contact Enslow Publishing, New York, New York, at 1-800-398-2504.

Find us on

Contents

Words in the glossary appear in **bold** type
the first time they are used in the text.

A Well-Rounded Star

Zoë Kravitz was brought up in the world of show business. So it's no surprise that she chose to make a career of her own in the **industry**. Unlike many other stars, Zoë didn't just pick one area in show business to work in. She's an actress, a musician, a model, and even a producer, or a person who oversees and often helps to pay for the making of a movie or TV show.

In addition to Zoë's **professional** work, she also supports important causes and speaks out about issues she cares about, such as the Black Lives Matter movement.

EVEN EARLY ON IN HER CAREER, ZOË WORKED IN DIFFERENT AREAS OF SHOW BUSINESS. ONE OF HER FIRST PARTS WAS IN A JAY-Z MUSIC VIDEO. SHE WAS ALSO A MODEL FOR A VERA WANG PERFUME.

Fame in the Family

Zoë was born on December 1, 1988, in Los Angeles, California. She comes from a famous family. Some might say a talent for music and acting was in her blood. Zoë's father is a famous rock musician named Lenny Kravitz. He's won several Grammy Awards for his music. Her mother is Lisa Bonet, a famous actress who has starred in many popular movies and TV shows.

FACTS BEHIND THE FIGURE

At first, Zoë's parents didn't want her working on movies or TV shows until she finished high school, but they later changed their minds. Zoë's first two movies came out in 2007—the same year she graduated high school.

Lenny Kravitz

Lisa Bonet

ZOË'S PARENTS SPLIT UP WHEN SHE WAS TWO, BUT SHE SPENT TIME LIVING WITH BOTH PARENTS THROUGHOUT HER CHILDHOOD.

Zoë started taking acting classes while she was a kid. She started working on her first two movies—*No Reservations* and *The Brave One*—while she was in her last year of high school.

The Start of a Star

Most of Zoë's early acting roles, or parts, were for supporting characters. These are people in the story who aren't the main characters. While she wasn't always playing the lead, many of Zoë's early movies were still successful and helped to put her on the map.

FACTS BEHIND THE FIGURE

Zoë is both Jewish and Black, as are both of her parents. She has said that she's been turned down for roles—especially lead roles—because she's Black. Today, Zoë often speaks out about the lack of representation for people of color in movies and TV.

EVEN AFTER APPEARING IN *X-MEN: FIRST CLASS*, ZOË STRUGGLED TO GET PARTS IN MOVIES. SHE OFTEN TRIED OUT AND GOT TURNED DOWN.

In 2011, she played a character named Angel who uses her insect-like wings to fly in *X-Men: First Class*. Part of the popular X-Men **franchise**, this movie gave Zoë what many consider to be her first big break in acting. Her performance in the movie even landed her a **nomination** for a Teen Choice Award!

In 2014, Zoë played a character named Christina in the movie *Divergent*. This movie was part of a trilogy, or group of three works, based on books by Veronica Roth. Zoë went on to play Christina again in the following movies in the trilogy, *Insurgent* and *Allegiant*.

FACTS BEHIND THE FIGURE

In addition to acting on screen, Zoë has lent her voice to several **animated** films. In 2017, she voiced Catwoman in *The Lego Batman Movie*. The following year, she was the voice of Mary Jane in *Spider-Man: Into the Spider-Verse*.

SEVERAL OF ZOË'S EARLY FILMS WERE ACTION MOVIES, INCLUDING *MAD MAX: FURY ROAD.*

In 2015, Zoë appeared in the popular and award-winning movie *Mad Max: Fury Road*. The next year, she played Leta Lestrange in *Fantastic Beasts and Where to Find Them*, the first in a series of **prequels** to the Harry Potter films. By now, her talent and skill for acting were clear.

11

Making Time for Music

With all the on-screen roles she's had, it might seem like Zoë's focus is totally on acting. But she also has a successful music career!

Zoë has been making music since she was a teenager. In 2014, her band Lolawolf released its first album. Zoë sings in the band and writes much of the music. The band's style is called electro-pop. This is a type of music that combines **characteristics** of electronic music with those of pop music.

In addition to her work with Lolawolf, Zoë has been featured singing on songs with several other artists, including Drake and Janelle Monáe.

THE BAND LOLAWOLF IS NAMED AFTER
ZOË'S YOUNGER BROTHER AND SISTER.
IT COMBINES THEIR NAMES: LOLA AND NAKOA-WOLF.

In Her Own Words
"With acting, I get **employed**. It's a job.
I have to be places at certain times.
Lolawolf is what I choose to do
with my free time."

On TV

By 2017, Zoë was, of course, no stranger to acting. However, besides a few small roles, she hadn't done much TV acting. That changed when she was cast in the HBO show *Big Little Lies*. In the show, she appeared alongside some big stars, such as Reese Witherspoon and Nicole Kidman. While Zoë's character on *Big Little Lies* was important to the show, she was not the star.

For her next TV project, Zoë was ready to take the lead. She was cast as the lead character in the Hulu series *High Fidelity*, which came out in 2020.

THE TV SHOW *HIGH FIDELITY* WAS BASED ON A 1995 BOOK OF THE SAME NAME. IN 2000, ZOË'S MOM, LISA BONET, ACTED IN THE MOVIE *HIGH FIDELITY*, ALSO BASED ON THE BOOK.

In Her Own Words

"As someone who's played so many supporting roles, I wanted to make sure that all the characters (in *High Fidelity*) felt **multidimensional** ... Unless you have characters that people want to hang out with, nobody's going to watch the show."

IT WAS ZOË'S IDEA TO HAVE THE SHOW BE BASED IN BROOKLYN. IT WAS ORIGINALLY SUPPOSED TO TAKE PLACE IN LOS ANGELES, CALIFORNIA.

Zoë has said she is a fan of both the book and movie that her show *High Fidelity* was based on. In the Hulu show, Zoë played the owner of a record store in Brooklyn, New York. As of 2020, Brooklyn is where Zoë lives in real life too. This, along with Zoë's passion for music, helped Zoë relate to her character on the show.

Zoë not only starred in *High Fidelity*, she also helped produce it. As a producer, she had more say in what happened on the show than she would have if she were only an actor in it.

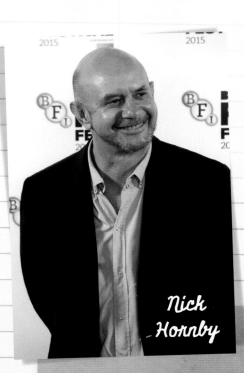

Nick Hornby

FACTS BEHIND THE FIGURE

Zoë was one of several producers on *High Fidelity*. Another was Nick Hornby, author of the book the show was based on.

Cast as Catwoman

In October 2019, Zoë Kravitz fans got some big news. The star was set to play Selina Kyle—also known as Catwoman—in the film *The Batman*. Zoë stars in the movie with Robert Pattinson, who plays Bruce Wayne, or Batman.

FACTS BEHIND THE FIGURE

Zoë began working on *The Batman* in early 2020. However, filming came to a halt for several months due to the COVID-19 **pandemic**.

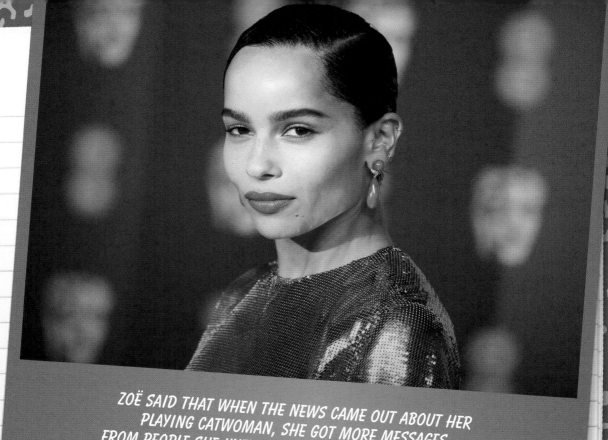

ZOË SAID THAT WHEN THE NEWS CAME OUT ABOUT HER PLAYING CATWOMAN, SHE GOT MORE MESSAGES FROM PEOPLE SHE KNEW THAN SHE DID ON HER BIRTHDAY!

While Zoë was certainly well known and successful in her acting career before being cast as Catwoman, starring in a Batman movie is a new level of fame. The Batman universe has a huge fanbase. Zoë has said that she never thought she'd have such an important role in such a big production.

What's Next?

When it was announced that Zoë would be in *The Batman*, she was already familiar with playing Catwoman. However, starring in a live-action movie is pretty different from voicing the character in an animated film, like she did in *The Lego Batman Movie*.

Whether she's starring on the big screen or singing with her band in front of screaming fans, one thing is for sure: Zoë Kravitz is a serious star—one whose career is likely only just beginning to take off. Whatever comes next for Zoë, it's sure to be exciting!

Zoë's Timeline

1988: ZOË IS BORN ON DECEMBER 1.

2007: ZOË'S FIRST TWO MOVIES, *NO RESERVATIONS* AND *THE BRAVE ONE,* COME OUT.

2011: ZOË APPEARS IN *X-MEN: FIRST CLASS.*

2014: ZOË PLAYS CHRISTINA IN *DIVERGENT.*

LOLAWOLF RELEASES ITS FIRST ALBUM.

2015: *INSURGENT,* A FOLLOW-UP TO *DIVERGENT,* COMES OUT.

ZOË APPEARS IN THE MOVIE *MAD MAX: FURY ROAD.*

2016: THE FINAL *DIVERGENT* MOVIE, *ALLEGIANT,* COMES OUT.

ZOË IS IN *FANTASTIC BEASTS AND WHERE TO FIND THEM.*

2017: ZOË VOICES CATWOMAN IN *THE LEGO BATMAN MOVIE.*

ZOË IS IN THE TV SHOW *BIG LITTLE LIES.*

2019: IT IS ANNOUNCED THAT ZOË WILL PLAY CATWOMAN IN *THE BATMAN.*

2020: *HIGH FIDELITY* COMES OUT.

LOLAWOLF RELEASES A NEW ALBUM, CALLED *TENDERNESS.*

Glossary

animated Consisting of drawings or computer images that appear to move.

characteristic A quality that makes something different from other things.

employ To give a job to someone and pay them for their work.

franchise A series of related works that each include the same characters or different characters understood to exist in the same fictional universe.

industry A group of businesses or people providing a similar service.

multidimensional Having many aspects.

nomination A suggestion for an honor.

pandemic An occurrence in which a disease spreads very quickly and affects a large number of people over a wide area.

prequel A story that tells what happened before another story.

professional Having to do with a job someone does for a living.

For More Information

Books

McAneney, Caitie. *Gareth's Guide to Becoming a Pop Star*. New York, NY: Gareth Stevens Publishing, 2018.

Wood, Alix. *Be an Actor*. New York, NY: PowerKids Press, 2018.

Websites

Catwoman
www.dccomics.com/characters/catwoman
Find out more about Catwoman, the character Zoë plays in *The Batman*.

Zoë Kravitz Facts for Kids
kids.kiddle.co/Zo%C3%AB_Kravitz
Find out more about Zoë here.

★ Index ★